MW01675107

ENCOURAGEMENT for WOMEN

Timeless Words for Living Well

compiled by Becky Warner

Harold Shaw Publishers
Wheaton, Illinois

Compiled by Becky Warner

ISBN 0-87788-216-9

Cover photo © 1995 by Luci Shaw

02 01 00 99 98 97 96 95

10 9 8 7 6 5 4 3 2 1

Printed in Colombia.
Impreso en Colombia.

Many, O LORD my God,
are the wonders you have done.
The things you planned for us
no one can recount to you;
were I to speak and tell of them,
they would be too many
to declare.

Psalm 40:5, NIV

Grateful acknowledgment is made to the publishers of the Scripture versions, portions of which are quoted in this book, using the following abbreviations:

KJV	King James Version
NASB	New American Standard Bible
NKJV	New King James Version
NRSVB	New Revised Standard Version Bible
NIV	New International Version
RSV	Revised Standard Version
TLB	The Living Bible

Contents

Introduction 7
Who I Am in God's Eyes 9
Building Relationships 16
Trusting God's Provision 21
Meaningful Work 27
Guarding the Heart 31
Becoming More Like Christ 37
Faithful Stewardship 44
Home and Family 54
Pressing On 60
Present and Future Hope 66

Introduction

What does my future hold? Who am I in God's eyes? How can I become more like Christ in my relationships, my attitudes, and my work? And how can I keep going when I become so tired? This small book contains portions from the Bible that answer these questions and give us the encouragement we need to keep pressing forward. God's Word, with its guidance and promises, reminds us that his love and support are with us all the way as we discover and experience the fullness and goodness of life as he intends it.

Note: In order to speak more directly to women, we have used inclusive language where appropriate and accurate renderings can be made.

WHO I AM IN GOD'S EYES

The highest pinnacle of the spiritual life is not joy in unbroken sunshine but absolute and undoubting trust in the love of God.
A. W. Thorold

Why on earth am I worried about how I can be somebody? I am somebody, a unique creation of God.
Sarah Gudschinsky

God created humankind in His own image, in the image of God He created him; male and female He created them.
Genesis 1:27, NASB

For the LORD your God is he that goeth with you, to fight for you against your enemies, to save you.
Deuteronomy 20:4, KJV

O Lord my God, many and many a time you have done great miracles for us, and we are ever in your thoughts.
Psalm 40:5, TLB

For you created my inmost being; you knit me together in my mother's womb. I praise you because I am fearfully and wonderfully made; your works are wonderful, I know that full well. My frame was not hidden from you when I was made in the secret place.

When I was woven together in the depths of the earth, your eyes saw my unformed body. All the days ordained for me were written in your book before one of them came to be.
Psalm 139:13-16, NIV

But now thus saith the LORD that created thee, O Jacob, and he that formed thee, O Israel, Fear not: for I have redeemed thee, I have called thee by thy name; thou art mine.
Isaiah 43:1, KJV

Thus says the LORD, . . . "You are precious in My sight, . . . I love you."
Isaiah 43:4, NASB

"You will seek me and find me when you seek me with all your heart. I will be found by you," declares the LORD.
Jeremiah 29:13-14, NIV

Indeed, the very hairs of your head are all numbered. Do not fear; you are of more value than many sparrows.
Luke 12:7, NASB

But as many as received Him, to them He gave the right to become children of God, even to those who believe in His name.
John 1:12, NASB

For God so loved the world, that He gave His only begotten Son, that whoever believes in Him should not perish, but have eternal life.
John 3:16, NASB

Just as the Father has loved Me, I have also loved you; abide in My love.
John 15:9, NASB

We are able to hold our heads high no matter what happens and know that

all is well, for we know how dearly God loves us, and we feel this warm love everywhere within us because God has given us the Holy Spirit to fill our hearts with his love.
Romans 5:5, TLB

The Spirit himself testifies with our spirit that we are God's children.
Romans 8:16, NIV

I am convinced that neither death, nor life, nor angels, nor principalities, nor things present, nor things to come, nor powers, nor height, nor depth, nor any other created thing, shall be able to separate us from the love of God, which is in Christ Jesus our Lord.
Romans 8:38-39, NASB

For ye are all the children of God by faith in Christ Jesus.
Galatians 3:26, KJV

You are no longer foreigners and aliens, but fellow citizens with God's people and members of God's household.
Ephesians 2:19, NIV

What are human beings that you are mindful of them, or mortals, that you care for them? You made them for a little while lower than the angels; you have crowned them with glory and honor, subjecting all things under their feet.
Hebrews 2:6-8, NRSVB

You are a chosen people, a royal priesthood, a holy nation, a people belonging to God, that you may declare the praises of him who called you out of darkness into his wonderful light.
1 Peter 2:9, NIV

See how great a love the Father has bestowed upon us, that we should be called children of God; and such we are. For this reason the world does not know us, because it did not know Him.
1 John 3:1, NASB

BUILDING RELATIONSHIPS

Relating to one another is neither trivial nor simple, yet healthy relationships are what make our lives rich and full and good. It is the broken relationships that render us impoverished, sad, and empty. Most of our tears are shed over relationships. Knowing this, some people try to avoid close relationships in order to avoid tears, but they only end up being less human. God is always wanting to wash his love over our relationships, to flood them with grace. He took the risk of love; he wants us to do the same.

Gladys Hunt

Some friends play at friendship but a true friend sticks closer than one's nearest kin.
Proverbs 18:24, NRSV

Never abandon a friend—either yours or your father's. Then you won't need to go to a distant relative for help in your time of need.
Proverbs 27:10, TLB

Two are better than one because they have a good return for their labor. For if either of them falls, the one will lift up his companion. But woe to the one who falls when there is not another to lift him up.
Ecclesiastes 4:9-10, NASB

Therefore whatever you want others to do for you, do for them, for this is the Law and the Prophets.
Matthew 7:12, NASB

If therefore you are presenting your offering at the altar, and there remember that your brother has something against you, leave your offering there before the altar, and go your way, first be reconciled to your brother, and then come and present your offering.
Matthew 5:23-24, NASB

My command is this: Love each other as I have loved you.
John 15:12, NIV

The important thing for us as Christians is not what we eat or drink but stirring up goodness and peace and joy from the Holy Spirit. If you let Christ be Lord in these affairs, God will be glad; and so will others. In this way aim for harmony in the church and try to build each other up.
Romans 14:17-19, TLB

May God who gives patience, steadiness, and encouragement help you to live in complete harmony with each other—each with the attitude of Christ toward the other. And then all of us can praise the Lord together with one voice.
Romans 15:5-6, TLB

Bear one another's burdens, and thus fulfil the law of Christ.
Galatians 6:2, NASB

Learn to put aside your own desires so that you will become patient and godly, gladly letting God have his way with you. This will make possible the next step, which is for you to enjoy other people and to like them, and finally you will grow to love them deeply.
2 Peter 1:6-7, TLB

Be humble and gentle. Be patient with each other, making allowance for each other's faults because of your love. Try always to be led along together by the Holy Spirit, and so be at peace with one another.
Ephesians 4:2-3, TLB

Be kind to one another, tender-hearted, forgiving each another, just as God in Christ also has forgiven you.
Ephesians 4:32, NASB

Be patient with everyone. Make sure that nobody pays back wrong for wrong, but always try to be kind to each other and to everyone else.
1 Thessalonians 5:14-15, NIV

TRUSTING GOD'S PROVISION

Just about the time you think you can make both ends meet, somebody moves the ends.

Pansy Penner

It is the LORD who goes before you; he will be with you, he will not fail you or forsake you; do not fear or be dismayed.
Deuteronomy 31:8, RSV

For forty years you sustained them in the desert; they lacked nothing, their clothes did not wear out nor did their feet become swollen.
Nehemiah 9:21, NIV

All those who know your mercy, Lord, will count on you for help. For you have never yet forsaken those who trust in you.
Psalm 9:10, TLB

The young lions do lack and suffer hunger; but they who seek the LORD shall not be in want of any good thing.
Psalm 34:10, NASB

The LORD is my shepherd, I shall not be in want.
Psalm 23:1, NIV

Trust in the LORD, and do good; so shalt thou dwell in the land, and verily thou shalt be fed.
Psalm 37:3, KJV

For the LORD is good and his love endures forever; his faithfulness continues through all generations.
Psalm 100:5, NIV

He has satisfied the thirsty soul, and the hungry soul He has filled with what is good.
Psalm 107:9, NASB

When my spirit grows faint within me, it is you who know my way.
Psalm 142:3, NIV

The fear of others lays a snare, but one who trusts in the LORD is secure.
Proverbs 29:25, NRSVB

And ye shall eat in plenty, and be satisfied, and praise the name of the Lord your God, that hath dealt wondrously with you: and my people shall never be ashamed.
Joel 2:26, KJV

Ask the LORD for rain in the springtime; it is the LORD who makes the storm clouds. He gives showers of rain to you, and plants of the field to everyone.
Zechariah 10:1, NIV

Your Father knows what you need before you ask him.
Matthew 6:8, NIV

Ask and it will be given to you; seek and you will find; knock and the door will be opened to you. For everyone who asks receives; he who seeks finds; and to him who knocks, the door will be opened.
Matthew 7:7-8, NIV

Do not set your heart on what you will eat or drink; do not worry about it. For the pagan world runs after all such things, and your Father knows that you need them. But seek his kingdom, and these things will be given to you as well.
Luke 12:29-31, NIV

God is able to provide you with every blessing in abundance, so that you may always have enough of everything and may provide in abundance for every good work.
2 Corinthians 9:8, RSV

Do not be anxious about anything, but in everything, by prayer and petition, with thanksgiving, present your requests to God. And the peace of God, which transcends all understanding, will guard your hearts and your minds in Christ Jesus.
Philippians 4:6-7, NIV

But godliness with contentment is great gain.
1 Timothy 6:6, KJV

Let your conversation be without covetousness; and be content with such things as ye have: for he hath said, I will never leave thee, nor forsake thee.
Hebrews 13:5, KJV

And this is the confidence which we have before Him, that, if we ask anything according to His will, He hears us.
1 John 5:14, NASB

MEANINGFUL WORK

As we see how Esther served her generation according to the will of God, so our imagination is aroused to see how we might serve ours.

Miriam Adeney

Commit everything you do to the Lord. Trust him to help you do it and he will.
Psalm 37:5, TLB

The wicked earn no real gain, but those who sow righteousness get a true reward.
Proverbs 11:18, NRSVB

Hard work means prosperity; only a fool idles away his time.
Proverbs 12:11, TLB

All hard work brings a profit, but mere talk leads only to poverty.
Proverbs 14:23, NIV

Whatever your hand finds to do, do it with all your might, for in the grave, where you are going, there is neither working nor planning nor knowledge nor wisdom.
Ecclesiastes 9:10, NIV

Commit to the LORD whatever you do, and your plans will succeed.
Proverbs 16:3, NIV

God shall bring every work into judgment, with every secret thing, whether it be good, or whether it be evil.
Ecclesiastes 12:14, KJV

Then the King will say to those on His right hand, "Come, you blessed of my Father, inherit the kingdom prepared for you from the foundation of the world: for I was hungry and you gave Me food; I was thirsty and you gave Me drink; I was a stranger and you took Me in; I was naked and you clothed Me; I was sick and you visited Me; I was in prison and you came to Me. . . . Inasmuch as you did it to one of the least of these My brethren, you did it to Me.
Matthew 25:34-36, 40, NKJV

The one who wants to do right will get a rich reward. But the one who wants to get rich quick will quickly fail.
Proverbs 28:20, TLB

Never be lacking in zeal, but keep your spiritual fervor, serving the Lord.
Romans 12:11, NIV

Whatever you do, work at it with all your heart, as working for the Lord, not for others, since you know that you will receive an inheritance from the Lord as a reward. It is the Lord Christ you are serving.
Colossians 3:23-24, NIV

Work hard so God can say to you, "Well done." Be a good worker, one who does not need to be ashamed when God examines your work. Know what his Word says and means.
2 Timothy 2:15, TLB

GUARDING THE HEART

The people I know who truly like themselves as persons apart from their roles in life as husband, wife, parent, or job-holder, are those who have learned to be honest with themselves and who to some degree understand themselves. . . . Honesty with oneself, with God, and with one's fellow man is the first all-important step in spiritual and emotional growth.

Cecil G. Osborne

What doth the LORD thy God require of thee, but to fear the LORD thy God, to walk in all his ways, and to love him, and to serve the LORD thy God with all thy heart and with all thy soul.
Deuteronomy 10:12, KJV

The LORD does not look at the things people look at. They look at the outward appearance, but the LORD looks at the heart.
1 Samuel 16:7, NIV

Happy are those who do not follow the advice of the wicked, or take the path that sinners tread, . . . but their delight is in the law of the Lord, and on his law they meditate day and night.
Psalm 1:1-2, NRSVB

Search me, O God, and know my heart; try me and know my anxious thoughts; and see if there be any hurtful

way in me, and lead me in the everlasting way.
Psalm 139:23-24, NASB

Do not be wise in your own eyes; fear the Lord and turn away from evil.
Proverbs 3:7, NASB

The person of integrity walks securely, but one who takes crooked paths will be found out.
Proverbs 10:9, NIV

Truthful lips endure forever, but a lying tongue lasts only a moment.
Proverbs 12:19, NIV

Do not wear yourself out to get rich; have the wisdom to show restraint. Cast but a glance at riches, and they are gone, for they will surely sprout wings and fly off to the sky like an eagle.
Proverbs 23:4-5, NIV

Stand at the crossroads and look; ask for the ancient paths, ask where the good way is, and walk in it, and you will find rest for your souls.
Jeremiah 6:16, NIV

Let us examine and probe our ways, and let us return to the LORD.
Lamentations 3:40, NASB

Do not store up for yourselves treasures on earth, where moth and rust destroy, and where thieves break in and steal. But store up for yourselves treasures in heaven, where moth and rust do not destroy, and where thieves do not break in and steal. For where your treasure is, there your heart will be also.
Matthew 6:19-21, NIV

"Love the Lord your God with all your heart, and with all your soul and with

all your mind." This is the first and greatest commandment. And the second is like it: "Love your neighbor as yourself."
Matthew 22:37-39, NIV

Test yourselves to see if you are in the faith; examine yourselves! Or do you not recognize this about yourselves, that Jesus Christ is in you?
2 Corinthians 13:5, NASB

Whatever is true, whatever is noble, whatever is right, whatever is pure, whatever is lovely, whatever is admirable—if anything is excellent or praiseworthy—think about such things.
Philippians 4:8, NIV

Because he himself suffered when he was tempted, he is able to help those who are being tempted.
Hebrews 2:18, NIV

If we are living in the light of God's presence, just as Christ does, then we have wonderful fellowship and joy with each other, and the blood of Jesus his Son cleanses us from every sin.
1 John 1:7, TLB

Do not love the world or the things in the world. The love of the Father is not in those who love the world; for all that is in the world—the desire of the flesh, the desire of the eyes, the pride in riches—comes not from the Father but from the world. And the world and its desire are passing away, but those who do the will of God live forever.
1 John 2:15-17, NRSVB

BECOMING MORE LIKE CHRIST

Fill me with your love
Your radiance
Your wisdom and power.
Make my life the proof
Of the truth I proclaim.
I am not content, dear Lord
Simply to impart information.
I long to behold transformation.
Ruth Harmes Calkin

A gracious woman retains honor.
Proverbs 11:16, NKJV

Charm is deceitful and beauty is vain, but a woman who fears the LORD, she shall be praised.
Proverbs 31:30, NKJV

But I say unto you, Love your enemies, bless them that curse you, do good to them that hate you, and pray for them which despitefully use you, and persecute you; that ye may be the children of your Father which is in heaven: for he maketh his sun to rise on the evil and on the good, and sendeth rain on the just and on the unjust.
Matthew 5:44-45, KJV

If any want to become my followers, let them deny themselves and take up their cross daily and follow me. For those who want to save their life will

lose it, and those who lose their life for my sake will save it. What does it profit them if they gain the whole world, but lose or forfeit themselves?
Luke 9:23-25, NRSVB

If you hold to my teaching, you are really my disciples. Then you will know the truth, and the truth will set you free.
John 8:31-32, NIV

Now that I, your Lord and Teacher, have washed your feet, you also should wash one another's feet.
John 13:14, NIV

A new commandment I give you: Love one another. As I have loved you, so you must love one another. Everyone will know that you are my disciples if you love one another.
John 13:34-35, NIV

We Christians . . . can be mirrors that brightly reflect the glory of the Lord. And as the Spirit of the Lord works within us, we become more and more like him.
2 Corinthians 3:18, TLB

When the Holy Spirit controls our lives he will produce this kind of fruit in us: love, joy, peace, patience, kindness, goodness, faithfulness, gentleness and self-control.
Galatians 5:22, TLB

Let us not become weary in doing good, for at the proper time we will reap a harvest if we do not give up. Therefore, as we have opportunity, let us do good to all people.
Galatians 6:9-10, NIV

Be full of love for others, following the example of Christ who loved you and gave himself to God as a sacrifice to take away your sins.
Ephesians 5:2, TLB

Being filled with the fruits of righteousness, which are by Jesus Christ, unto the glory and praise of God.
Philippians 1:11, KJV

Put on then, as God's chosen ones, holy and beloved, compassion, kindness, lowliness, meekness, and patience, forbearing one another and, if one has a complaint against another, forgiving each other; as the Lord has forgiven you, so you also must forgive.
Colossians 3:12-13, RSV

Do everything without complaining or arguing, so that you may become blameless and pure, children of God without fault in a crooked and depraved generation, in which you shine like stars in the universe as you hold out the word of life.
Philippians 2:14-16, NIV

And whatever you do or say, let it be as a representative of the Lord Jesus, and come with him into the presence of God the Father to give him your thanks.
Colossians 3:17, TLB

The Lord's servant must not be quarrelsome but kindly to every one, an apt teacher, forbearing, correcting his opponents with gentleness. God may perhaps grant that they will repent and come to know the truth.
2 Timothy 2:24-25, RSV

If any of you is lacking wisdom, ask God, who gives to all generously and ungrudgingly, and it will be given you. But ask in faith, never doubting, for the one who doubts is like a wave of the sea, driven and tossed by the wind.
James 1:5-6, NRSVB

All of you serve each other with humble spirits, for God gives special blessings to those who are humble, but sets himself against those who are proud. If you will humble yourselves under the mighty hand of God, in his good time he will lift you up.
1 Peter 5:5-6, TLB

Let us love one another, for love comes from God. Everyone who loves has been born of God and knows God. . . . Dear friends, since God so loved us, we also ought to love one another.
1 John 4:7, 11, NIV

FAITHFUL STEWARDSHIP

Why do we say no? In order to say yes to what really matters.
Miriam Adeney

Know the God of your father, and serve Him with a whole heart and a willing mind; for the LORD searches all hearts, and understands every intent of the thoughts.
1 Chronicles 28:9, NASB

The wicked borrows and does not pay back, but the righteous is gracious and gives.
Psalm 37:21, NASB

Happy are those who consider the poor, the LORD delivers them in the day of trouble. The LORD protects them and keeps them alive; they are called happy in the land.
Psalm 41:1-2, NRSVB

A wise person thinks ahead; a fool doesn't, and even brags about it!
Proverbs 13:16, TLB

Honor the Lord from your wealth, and from the first of all your produce; so your barns will be filled with plenty, and your vats will overflow with new wine.
Proverbs 3:9-10, NASB

Blessed are those who hear the word of God, and observe it.
Luke 11:28, NASB

If you give, you will get! Your gift will return to you in full and overflowing measure, pressed down, shaken together to make room for more, and running over. Whatever measure you use to give—large or small—will be used to measure what is given back to you.
Luke 6:38, TLB

One who is faithful in a very little thing is faithful also in much; and one who is unrighteous in a very little

thing is unrighteous also in much. If therefore you have not been faithful in the use of unrighteous Mammon, who will entrust the true riches to you?
Luke 16:10-11, NASB

How hard it is for those who are wealthy to enter the kingdom of God! For it is easier for a camel to go through the eye of a needle, than for a rich person to enter the kingdom of God.
Luke 18:24-25, NASB

No one can serve two masters; for either they will hate the one and love the other, or they will hold to one and despise the other. You cannot serve God and Mammon.
Matthew 6:24, NASB

If you love Me, you will keep My commandments.
John 14:15, NASB

In everything I showed you that by working hard in this manner you must help the weak and remember the words of the Lord Jesus, that He Himself said, "It is more blessed to give than to receive."
Acts 20:35, NASB

Let others regard us in this manner, as servants of Christ, and stewards of the mysteries of God. In this case, moreover, it is required of stewards that one be found trustworthy.
1 Corinthians 4:1-2, NASB

Whether, then, you eat or drink or whatever you do, do all to the glory of God.
1 Corinthians 10:31, NASB

For you know the grace of our Lord Jesus Christ, that though He was rich,

yet for your sake He became poor, that you through His poverty might become rich.
2 Corinthians 8:9, NASB

The one who sows sparingly will also reap sparingly, and the one who sows bountifully will also reap bountifully. Each of you must give as you have made up your mind, not reluctantly or under compulsion, for God loves a cheerful giver.
2 Corinthians 9:6-7, NRSVB

Let those who steal steal no longer; but rather let them labor, performing with their own hands what is good, in order that they may have something to share with anyone who has need.
Ephesians 4:28, NASB

Those who want to get rich fall into temptation and a snare and many foolish and harmful desires which plunge men into ruin and destruction. For the love of money is a root of all sorts of evil, and some by longing for it have wandered away from the faith, and pierced themselves with many a pang. But flee from these things . . . and pursue righteousness, godliness, faith, love, perseverance and gentleness.
1 Timothy 6:9-11, NASB

For God is not unjust so as to forget your work and the love which you have shown toward His name, in having ministered and in still ministering to the saints.
Hebrews 6:10, NASB

When God's children are in need, you be the one to help them out. And get into the habit of inviting guests home

for dinner or, if they need lodging, for the night.
Romans 12:13, TLB

Do not forget to entertain strangers, for by so doing some people have entertained angels without knowing it.
Hebrews 13:1-2, NIV

And do not neglect doing good and sharing; for with such sacrifices God is pleased.
Hebrews 13:16, NASB

For if any are hearers of the word and not doers, they are like those who look at themselves in a mirror; for they look at themselves and, on going away, immediately forget what they were like. But those who look into the perfect law, the lawof liberty, and persevere, . . . they will be blessed in their doing.
James 1:23-25, NRSVB

Cheerfully share your home with those who need a meal or a place to stay for the night. God has given each of you some special abilities; be sure to use them to help each other, passing on to others God's many kinds of blessings.
1 Peter 4:9-10, TLB

Abide in Him, so that if He should appear, we may have confidence and not shrink away from Him in shame at His coming.
1 John 2:28, NASB

But whoever has the world's goods, and beholds someone in need and closes their heart against him, how does the love of God abide in them? Little children, let us not love with word or with tongue, but in deed and truth. We shall know by this that we are of the truth, and shall assure our heart before Him.

1 John 3:17-19, NASB

HOME AND FAMILY

Unity and diversity. Form and freedom. Togetherness and individuality. A family.
Edith Schaeffer

A happy family is but an earlier heaven.
Sir John Browning

Honor your father and your mother, that your days may be long in the land which the LORD your God gives you.
Exodus 20:12, RSV

Cursed be anyone who dishonors his father or mother.
Deuteronomy 27:16, NRSVB

A true friend is always loyal, and a brother is born to help in time of need.
Proverbs 17:17, TLB

The father of the righteous will greatly rejoicc, and he who begets a wise son will be glad in him. Let your father and your mother be glad, and let her rejoice who gave birth to you.
Proverbs 23:24-25, NASB

By wisdom a house is built, and by understanding it is established; by knowledge the rooms are filled with all precious and pleasant riches.
Proverbs 24:3-4, RSV

Those who love me will keep my word, and my Father will love them, and we will come to them and make our home with them.
John 14:23, NRSVB

Instead, speaking the truth in love, we will in all things grow up into him who is the Head, that is, Christ.
Ephesians 4:15, NIV

Do not let any unwholesome talk come out of your mouths, but only what is helpful for building others up according to their needs, that it may benefit those who listen.
Ephesians 4:29, NIV

Therefore encourage one another, and build up one another, just as you also are doing.
1 Thessalonians 5:11, NASB

Therefore, whoever humbles himself like this child is the greatest in the kingdom of heaven. . . . See that you do not look down on one of these little ones. For I tell you that their angels in heaven always see the face of my Father in heaven.
Matthew 18:4, 10, NIV

Never speak sharply to an older man, but plead with him respectfully just as though he were your own father. Talk to the younger men as you would to much loved brothers. Treat the older women as mothers, and the girls as your sisters, thinking only pure thoughts about them.
1 Timothy 5:1-2, TLB

Everyone should be quick to listen, slow to speak, and slow to become angry, for our anger does not bring about the righteous life that God desires.
James 1:19-20, NIV

You should be like one happy family, full of sympathy toward each other, loving one another with tender hearts and humble minds.
1 Peter 3:8, TLB

Let us not love with word or with tongue, but in deed and truth.
1 John 3:18, NASB

Those who say, "I love God," and hate their brothers or sisters, are liars; for those who do not love a brother or sister whom they have seen, cannot love God who they have not seen. The

commandment we have from him is this: those who love God must love their brothers and sisters also.
1 John 4:20-21, NRSVB

PRESSING ON

The experiences of our lives, when we let God use them, become the mysterious and perfect preparation for the work He will give us to do.
Corrie ten Boom

Understand, therefore, that the Lord your God is the faithful God who for a thousand generations keeps his promises and constantly loves those who love him and who obey his commands.
Deuteronomy 7:9, TLB

When you go to war against your enemies and see horses and chariots and an army greater than yours, do not be afraid of them, because the LORD your God, who brought you up out of Egypt, will be with you. . . . Do not be faint-hearted or afraid; do not be terrified or give way to panic before them. For the LORD your God is the one who goes with you to fight for you against your enemies to give you victory.
Deuteronomy 20:1, 3-4, NIV

Do not be afraid or discouraged because of this vast army. For the battle is not yours, but God's. You will not have to fight this battle. Take up your positions; stand firm and see the deliverance the LORD will give you. . . . Do not be afraid; do not be discouraged.
2 Chronicles 20:15, 17, NIV

Wait on the LORD: be of good courage, and he shall strengthen thine heart: wait, I say, on the LORD.
Psalm 27:14, KJV

The LORD gives strength to his people; the LORD blesses his people with peace.
Psalm 29:11, NIV

For this God is our God for ever and ever: he will be our guide even unto death.
Psalm 48:14, KJV

Cast thy burden upon the Lord, and he shall sustain thee: he shall never suffer the righteous to be moved.
Psalm 55:22, KJV

You chart the path ahead of me, and tell me where to stop and rest. Every moment, you know where I am. You both precede and follow me, and place your hand of blessing on my head.
Psalm 139:3, 5, TLB

Do not be afraid of sudden panic, or of the ruin of the wicked, when it comes; for the Lord will be your confidence and will keep your foot from being caught.
Proverbs 3:25-26, RSV

Let us run with endurance the race that is set before us, looking to Jesus, the author and finisher of our faith.
Hebrews 12:1-2, NKJV

For the mountains shall depart, and the hills be removed; but my kindness shall not depart from thee, neither shall the covenant of my peace be removed, saith the Lord that hath mercy on thee.
Isaiah 54:10, KJV

Come unto me, all ye that labour and are heavy laden, and I will give you rest.
Matthew 11:28, KJV

These things I have spoken unto you, that in me ye might have peace. In the world ye shall have tribulation: but be of good cheer, I have overcome the world.
John 16:33, KJV

Watch ye, stand fast in the faith, . . . be strong.
1 Corinthians 16:13, KJV

I can do all things through Him who strengthens me.
Philippians 4:13, NASB

As ye have therefore received Christ Jesus the Lord, so walk ye in him: rooted and built up in him, and stablished in the faith, as ye have been taught, abounding therein with thanksgiving.
Colossians 2:6-7, KJV

Now may our Lord Jesus Christ Himself and God our Father, who has loved us and given us eternal comfort and good hope by grace, comfort and strengthen your hearts in every good work and word.
2 Thessalonians 2:16-17, NASB

PRESENT AND FUTURE HOPE

I said to the man who stood at the gate of the year: Give me a light that I may tread safely into the unknown. And he replied: Go out into the darkness, and put thine hand into the hand of God. That shall be to thee better than light and safer than a known way.

M. Louise Haskins

Yea, though I walk through the valley of the shadow of death, I will fear no evil: for thou art with me; thy rod and thy staff they comfort me.
Psalm 23:4, KJV

Be of good courage, and he shall strengthen your heart, all ye that hope in the LORD.
Psalm 31:24, KJV

God is our refuge and strength, a very present help in trouble. Therefore we will not fear, though the earth should change, and though the mountains slip into the heart of the sea; though its waters roar and foam, though the mountains quake at its swelling pride.
Psalm 46:1-3, NASB

You guide me with your counsel, and afterward you will take me into glory.
Psalm 73:24, NIV

Though I walk in the midst of trouble, Thou wilt revive me; Thou wilt stretch forth Thy hand against the wrath of my enemies, and Thy right hand will save me.
Psalm 138:7, NASB

There is surely a future hope for you, and your hope will not be cut off.
Proverbs 23:18, NIV

"For I know the plans I have for you," declares the LORD, "plans to prosper you and not to harm you, plans to give you hope and a future."
Jeremiah 29:11, NIV

Heaven and earth will pass away, but My words shall not pass away.
Matthew 24:35, NASB

Lo, I am with you alway, even unto the end of the world.
Matthew 28:20, KJV

"I tell you the truth," Jesus replied, "no one who has left home or brothers or sisters or mother or father or children or fields for me and the gospel will fail to receive a hundred times as much in this present age (homes, brothers, sisters, mothers, children and fields—and with them, persecutions) and in the age to come, eternal life."
Mark 10:29-30, NIV

In my Father's house are many mansions: if it were not so, I would have told you. I go to prepare a place for you.
John 14:2, KJV

For the wages of sin is death; but the gift of God is eternal life through Jesus Christ our Lord.
Romans 6:23, KJV

For I am convinced that neither death nor life, neither angels nor demons, neither the present nor the future, nor any powers, neither height nor depth, nor anything else in all creation, will be able to separate us from the love of God that is in Christ Jesus our Lord.
Romans 8:38-39, NIV

Our light affliction, which is but for a moment, worketh for us a far more exceeding and eternal weight of glory; while we look not at the things which are seen, but at the things which are not seen: for the things which are seen

are temporal; but the things which are not seen are eternal.
2 Corinthians 4:17-18, KJV

For the Lord himself will come down from heaven, with a loud command, with the voice of the archangel and with the trumpet call of God, and the dead in Christ will rise first. After that, we who are still alive and are left will be caught up with them in the clouds to meet the Lord in the air. And so we will be with the Lord forever. Therefore encourage each other with these words.
1 Thessalonians 4:16-18, NIV

Let us hold unswervingly to the hope we possess, for he who promised is faithful.
Hebrews 10:23, NIV

Therefore are they before the throne of God, and serve him day and night in his temple: and he that sitteth on the throne shall dwell among them. They shall hunger no more, neither thirst anymore; neither shall the sun light on them, nor any heat. For the Lamb which is in the midst of the throne shall feed them, and shall lead them unto living fountains of waters.
Revelation 7:15-17, KJV

God shall wipe away all tears from their eyes; and there shall be no more death, neither sorrow, nor crying, neither shall there be any more pain: for the former things are passed away. . . . Behold I make all things new.
Revelation 21:4-5, KJV